CW00542836

Jones

by Iain Gray

Lang**Syne**
PUBLISHING
WRITING *to* REMEMBER

LangSyne
PUBLISHING
WRITING *to* REMEMBER

79 Main Street, Newtongrange,
Midlothian EH22 4NA
Tel: 0131 344 0414   Fax: 0845 075 6085
E-mail: info@lang-syne.co.uk
www.langsyneshop.co.uk

Design by Dorothy Meikle
Printed by Printwell Ltd
© Lang Syne Publishers Ltd 2018

ISBN 978-1-85217-377-7

Jones

MOTTO:
Without God, without anything.

CREST:
A lion rampant.

NAME variations include:
Jonas
Jone

*Echoes of a far distant past
can still be found in most names*

Chapter one:

Origins of Scottish surnames

by George Forbes

It all began with the Normans.

For it was they who introduced surnames into common usage more than a thousand years ago, initially based on the title of their estates, local villages and chateaux in France to distinguish and identify these landholdings, usually acquired at the point of a bloodstained sword.

Such grand descriptions also helped enhance the prestige of these arrogant warlords and generally glorify their lofty positions high above the humble serfs slaving away below in the pecking order who only had single names, often with Biblical connotations as in Pierre and Jacques.

The only descriptive distinctions among this peasantry concerned their occupations, like Pierre the swineherd or Jacques the ferryman.

The Normans themselves were originally Vikings (or Northmen) who raided, colonised and eventually settled down around the French coastline.

They had sailed up the Seine in their longboats in 900 AD under their ferocious leader Rollo and ruled the roost in north east France before sailing over to conquer England, bringing their relatively new tradition of having surnames with them.

It took another hundred years for the Normans to percolate northwards and surnames did not begin to appear in Scotland until the thirteenth century.

These adventurous knights brought an aura of chivalry with them and it was said no damsel of any distinction would marry a man unless he had at least two names.

The family names included that of Scotland's great hero Robert De Brus and his compatriots were warriors from families like the De Morevils, De Umphravils, De Berkelais, De Quincis, De Viponts and De Vaux.

As the knights settled the boundaries of their vast estates, they took territorial names, as in Hamilton, Moray, Crawford, Cunningham, Dunbar, Ross, Wemyss, Dundas, Galloway, Renfrew, Greenhill, Hazelwood, Sandylands and Church-hill.

Other names, though not with any obvious geographical or topographical features, nevertheless derived from ancient parishes like Douglas, Forbes, Dalyell and Guthrie.

Other surnames were coined in connection with occupations, castles or legendary deeds. Stuart originated in the word steward, a prestigious post which was an integral part of any large medieval household. The same applied to Cooks, Chamberlains, Constables and Porters.

Borders towns and forts – needed in areas like the Debateable Lands which were constantly fought over by feuding local families – had their own distinctive names; and it was often from them that the resident groups took their communal titles, as in the Grahams of Annandale, the Elliots and Armstrongs of the East Marches, the Scotts and Kerrs of Teviotdale and Eskdale.

Even physical attributes crept into surnames, as in Small, Little and More (the latter being 'beg' in Gaelic), Long or Lang, Stark, Stout, Strong or Strang and even Jolly.

Mieklejohns would have had the strength of several men, while Littlejohn was named after the legendary sidekick of Robin Hood.

Colours got into the act with Black, White, Grey, Brown and Green (Red developed into Reid,

Ruddy or Ruddiman). Blue was rare and nobody ever wanted to be associated with yellow.

Pompous worthies took the name Wiseman, Goodman and Goodall.

Words intimating the sons of leading figures were soon affiliated into the language as in Johnson, Adamson, Richardson and Thomson, while the Norman equivalent of Fitz (from the French-Latin 'filius' meaning 'son') cropped up in Fitzmaurice and Fitzgerald.

The prefix 'Mac' was 'son of' in Gaelic and clans often originated with occupations – as in MacNab being sons of the Abbot, MacPherson and MacVicar being sons of the minister and MacIntosh being sons of the chief.

The church's influence could be found in the names Kirk, Clerk, Clarke, Bishop, Friar and Monk. Proctor came from a church official, Singer and Sangster from choristers, Gilchrist and Gillies from Christ's servant, Mitchell, Gilmory and Gilmour from servants of St Michael and Mary, Malcolm from a servant of Columba and Gillespie from a bishop's servant.

The rudimentary medical profession was represented by Barber (a trade which also once included dentistry and surgery) as well as Leech or Leitch.

Businessmen produced Merchants, Mercers, Monypennies, Chapmans, Sellers and Scales, while down at the old village watermill the names that cropped up included Miller, Walker and Fuller.

Other self explanatory trades included Coopers, Brands, Barkers, Tanners, Skinners, Brewsters and Brewers, Tailors, Saddlers, Wrights, Cartwrights, Smiths, Harpers, Joiners, Sawyers, Masons and Plumbers.

Even the scenery was utilised as in Craig, Moor, Hill, Glen, Wood and Forrest.

Rank, whether high or low, took its place with Laird, Barron, Knight, Tennant, Farmer, Husband, Granger, Grieve, Shepherd, Shearer and Fletcher.

The hunt and the chase supplied Hunter, Falconer, Fowler, Fox, Forrester, Archer and Spearman.

The renowned medieval historian Froissart, who eulogised about the romantic deeds of chivalry (and who condemned Scotland as being a poverty stricken wasteland), once sniffily dismissed the peasantry of his native France as the jacquerie (or the jacques-without-names) but it was these same humble folk who ended up overthrowing the arrogant aristocracy.

In the olden days, only the blueblooded knights of antiquity were entitled to full, proper names, both Christian and surnames, but with the passing of time and a more egalitarian, less feudal atmosphere, more respectful and worthy titles spread throughout the populace as a whole.

Echoes of a far distant past can still be found in most names and they can be borne with pride in commemoration of past generations who fought and toiled in some capacity or other to make our nation what it now is, for good or ill.

Chapter two:

Celtic connections

The most common name in Wales, the second most common in England and ranked 56th in Scotland, 'Jones' is a surname that means 'son of John', while in Wales it derives from 'Ioan', 'Ieuan' or 'Sion', all Welsh versions of 'John'.

The name John, in turn, derives from the Latin personal name 'Johannes', meaning 'Yahweh is gracious' – and with 'Yahweh' indicating 'God', that is why Jones is a name with truly religious connotations.

This may explain the Jones motto of 'Without God, without anything' – an English translation of the original Welsh 'Heb dduw, heb ddim'.

Although Jones and its variants is a name found in the English county of Huntingdonshire as early as 1279 and even earlier in the Denbighshire area of Wales – long before it appears in Scottish historical records – there are nevertheless intriguing and not commonly known links between Wales and southern Scotland.

From even before the Roman withdrawal from Britain in 407 AD, and until as late as the early

1300s, it was actually the Welsh, or Brythonic, language that flourished in southern Scotland.

This language has been identified and labelled by linguists as 'P-Celtic', as opposed to the 'Q-Celtic' of the Irish and those natives of Scotland who lived beyond the Highland Line.

It is from this linguistic distinction that the modern-day expression of 'minding your Ps and Qs' originates.

It was the P-Celtic speakers, identified as 'Britons', who formed the four tribes of southern Scotland – the Novantae in Galloway, the Votadini in Lothian, the Damnonii in the Clyde Valley and the Selgovae in the central Southern Uplands.

These tribes were known as the 'the Men of the North', to distinguish them from their fellow P-Celtic speakers who were settled further south – in Wales.

What is now the Scottish royal burgh of Dumbarton, known in P-Celtic as 'Dun Breatann' (the fortress of the Britons) served as the capital of what was the Welsh kingdom of Strathclyde.

Further evidence of the close link between the early Welsh – such as bearers of the Jones name – and Scotland can be found in one of the earliest written histories of southern Scotland.

Known as *The Gododdin*, it was written in the language of the Welsh.

Bearers of the Jones name, in its original Welsh forms of Ioan, Ieuan or Sion, also had a great deal in common with their Celtic counterparts in later centuries.

This was through the fact that in the late thirteenth century both nations fell prey to the dynastic and imperialistic ambitions of England's ruthless Edward I, who was determined to not only bring them under his domination but also to crush their Celtic identity.

Known in Welsh as Cymru, and with the motto of 'Cymru am byth' ('Wales Forever'), the nation was annexed to the English Crown in 1284.

This boiled over into rebellion in 1294, when Edward ordered the Welsh to join him in his territorial battles with France's Philip IV.

A national leader, in the same inspiring and heroic mould as his Scottish contemporaries William Wallace and the future warrior king Robert the Bruce, arose in the form of Madog ap Llywelyn of Merioneth, who inflicted a series of stunning defeats on Edward's occupying army.

But the rebellion was brutally crushed in March of 1295, and the nation fully subjugated.

Still burning with resentment over English domination of their nation, bearers of the Jones name and their fellow countrymen were nevertheless three years later among the ranks of the famed Welsh long-bowmen conscripted into Edward's ranks to crush a rebellion that had meanwhile spread like wildfire throughout Scotland.

Although these bowmen, wielding 6ft long bows whose iron-tipped arrows could pierce armour, contributed much to the defeat of the freedom fighter William Wallace at the battle of Falkirk of July 1298, Edward had always entertained serious doubts over their true loyalty.

Sixteen years later, at the battle of Bannockburn, when a Scots army commanded by Robert the Bruce decisively defeated an English army under Edward II, it is recorded that 'several thousand' Welsh bowmen and infantry who had been in his ranks managed to escape in the confused aftermath of the battle.

They are said to have made their way south to the safety of Carlisle, before making the journey southeastwards to their native Cymru.

In a much later conflict, part of which was fought on the high seas, John Paul Jones was the naval commander and hero of the American War of Independence of 1775 to 1783.

Born in 1747 on the Arbigland estate near Kirkbean, in the Stewarty of Kircudbright, on the southern coast of Scotland, this son of a humble gardener was destined to become recognised as 'Father of the American Navy', thanks to his daring naval exploits on behalf of his adopted country.

He first went to sea at the age of 13, sailing out of the northern English port of Whitehaven, later serving aboard a number of merchant ships and steadily rising through the ranks of command.

But, facing trial in 1772 for killing one of his crew in a dispute over wages, he fled to Fredericksburg, in Virginia, where his older brother who had settled there some years earlier had recently died.

It was some time after this that he adopted the name 'Jones' as his surname, having actually been born John Paul.

This was in honour of his friend the statesman Willie Jones, of Halifax, North Carolina, who had inspired him with his revolutionary views, and for whom present day Jones County in North Carolina is named.

On the outbreak of the American War of Independence, also known as the American Revolutionary War, Jones offered his services to the newly-established Continental Navy, soon to become known as the United States Navy, and was assigned to the rank of 1st Lieutenant.

A number of successful engagements against the British Navy followed, and on June 14, 1777, the memorable day on which the flag known as the Stars and Stripes was first adopted, he was given command of the fighting vessel *Ranger*.

Less than a year later, revolutionary France was in alliance with America, and it was from the French port of Brest that Captain John Paul Jones sailed in April of 1778 to launch attacks on the western coasts of Britain – most notably an assault on Whitehaven, the very port from which as a young lad he had embarked on his career at sea.

In August of the following year, in command of the *Bonhomme Richard* and in a furious engament with the British Navy off Flamborough Head, Jones uttered his famous "I have not yet begun to fight!" when the tide of battle appeared to be turning against him.

Following the conclusion of the war in 1783,

Jones found service with the Russian Navy for a time, eventually dying in Paris in July of 1792 showered with honours from America, France and Russia.

He was buried in the French capital, but his body was returned to America with great ceremony in 1906 and later re-interred in a bronze and marble sarcophagus in the Naval Academy Chapel in Annapolis.

In his original homeland, the cottage in which he was born on the Arbigland estate was restored in 1993 and houses a museum dedicated to the famous seafarer's colourful life and times.

Chapter three:

Honours and fame

From the high seas to the world of architecture, Inigo Jones, born in the Smithfield area of London in 1573, was the renowned architect responsible for some of the capital's earliest and most famous landmarks.

The son of a clothmaker, surprisingly little is known of his early life despite a fame that has endured to this day, but what is known is that it was when he was aged about 25 that he made the first of two visits to Italy to study its magnificent Renaissance architecture. Inspired by what he saw and studied, he returned to his native land and over the next few decades introduced the Renaissance style to the city of his birth.

Most notable examples of this are the Queen's House, at Greenwich, on which he started in 1616, the Banqueting House at Whitehall and the design of Covent Garden.

In addition to his work as an architect, Jones also turned his talents to stage design, working with such great English playwrights as Ben Jonson.

As Surveyor of Works to King Charles I, Jones, who died in 1652, also conducted the first detailed survey of the ancient group of standing stones in Wiltshire known as Stonehenge.

It was his detailed measurements of the mysterious neolithic site that revealed how it had been laid out with meticulous mathematical precision, leading future scholars to speculate that this may have been in order to align it with the movements of the sun and the moon.

From the seventeenth century to the nineteenth century, George Fowler Jones was the Scottish architect and early photographer who was born in Aberdeen in 1817 and who died in 1905.

His first major work involved repairs to the fire-damaged York Minster in the early 1840s, while other work he undertook throughout the length and breadth of the United Kingdom includes the Church of St Mary in Gosforth, Leeds, and renovations to Castle Grant, near Grantown-on-Spey, in Morayshire.

A friend of the pioneering photographer William Fox Talbot, inventor of the negative/positive process of photography, Jones was also a gifted photographer himself, and his large collection of photographs is now held in the National Media Museum, in Bradford.

It is not only in the fields of architecture and photography that bearers of the Jones name have distinguished themselves, but also in medicine.

Recognised as a pioneer of ophthalmology, as the study and treatment of the eye is known, Thomas Wharton Jones was the leading Scottish physiologist and ophthalmologist who was born in 1808 in St Andrews and who died in 1891.

After studying medicine, he worked as an assistant from 1827 to 1829 to the Edinburgh University anatomy lecturer Robert Knox, a period during which his promising career nearly came to an abrupt end when he became implicated in the case of the notorious body snatchers and murderers Burke and Hare.

Burke and Hare sold the freshly interred bodies they exhumed from graves – and of people they had themselves killed – to medical practitioners such as Jones and Knox, who would use them for medical research.

But Jones was cleared of having had any knowledge of their nefarious activities and, fortunately for posterity, went on to pursue his passion of the study of the eye, resulting in some of the first detailed anatomical drawings of the organ.

Appointed professor of ophthalmic medicine and surgery at University College, London, a post he held for thirty years, and a Fellow of the Royal College of Surgeons, his many publications include *The principles and practice of ophthalmic medicine and surgery*, first published in 1847.

Returning to the battlefield, Robert Digby-Jones was a posthumous Scottish recipient of the Victoria Cross, the highest award for bravery in the face of enemy action for British and Commonwealth forces.

Born in 1876 in Edinburgh, he was a lieutenant in the Corps of Royal Engineers during the South African War, also known as the Boer War, when, in January of 1900, during an attack on Wagon Hill, at Ladysmith, he and a trooper of the Imperial Light Horse led a force which managed to re-occupy the hill after Jones shot the enemy leader dead before he was also shot and killed.

His Victoria Cross is displayed at the Royal Engineers Museum in Chatham, England.

In more contemporary times, Lieutenant Colonel Herbert Jones, who was more familiarly known as 'H' Jones, was another posthumous recipient of the Victoria Cross.

Born in Putney in 1940, he was commanding

officer of 2 Battalion, Parachute Regiment, during Britain's war with Argentina known as the Falklands War, when, on May 28, 1982, he led an attack on enemy positions in an around the settlements of Darwin and Goose Green.

He was killed after seizing a machine-gun and single-handedly launching a charge on the enemy trenches.

In an earlier conflict, that of the Second World War, Professor Reginald Victor Jones, better known as Professor R.V. Jones, was the English physicist and expert in scientific military intelligence who is recognised as having played a vital role in Britain's defence.

Born in 1911, he served as assistant director of intelligence (science) to Britain's Air Ministry, and it was in this role that he helped to develop technologies that include 'chaff' – strips of aluminium foil dropped from aircraft to confuse enemy radar.

Known today as 'the father of scientific and technical intelligence', in 1993 he became the first recipient of the R.V. Jones Intelligence Award, created in his honour by America's CIA.

Author of *Most Secret War: British Scientific Intelligence 1939-45*, he died in 1997.

From heroes of warfare to heroes of a rather different order, John Luther Jones, born in 1863, was the American railroad engineer better known as Casey Jones.

Employed by the Illinois Central Railroad, it had been been on a rainy and foggy night in April of 1900, as his passenger train approached Vaughan, in Mississippi, that he and his fellow engine crew realised they were in danger of colliding with a stalled freight train.

The rest of the crew jumped overboard, but Casey remained to apply the brakes and lessen the force of the impact, as a result of which no one was killed or seriously injured.

All, that is, apart from Casey Jones himself, whose dead body was pulled from the twisted wreckage with his hand still clutched to the brake.

It was his friend and fellow railroad worker Wallace Saunders who later immortalised his brave actions in the popular *Ballad of Casey Jones*.

Chapter four:

On the world stage

Bearers of the proud name of Jones have excelled in a number of pursuits, not least in the world of entertainment.

From door-to-door vacuum cleaner salesman, builder's labourer and lorry driver to international star, **Tom Jones** is the Welsh singer who was born Thomas Jones Woodward in the small community of Pontypridd in 1941.

His first major hit was the 1965 *It's Not Unusual*, while in the same year he won a Grammy Award for Best New Artist.

A succession of hits have followed, including *Green Green Grass of Home*, from 1966, the 1968 *Delilah* and, from 1971, *She's a Lady*, while he received another major boost to his career in 1999 when the single *Sex Bomb* became his biggest hit to date.

The entertainer, who received a BRIT Award for Outstanding Contribution to Music in 2003, has, at the time of writing, sold in excess of 100 million records.

His wife Melinda, better known as Linda and to whom he had been married for 59 years, died in 2016.

The recipient of numerous awards, **Grace Jones** is the Jamaican-American singer, actress and model who was born Grace Mendoza in 1948 in Spanish Town, Jamaica.

Her top-selling albums include the 1977 *Portfolio* and the 2008 *Bulletproof Heart*, while films in which she has appeared include the 1985 *Conan the Destroyer* and the 1986 James Bond film, *A View to a Kill*.

Born in Chicago in 1933, **Quincy Jones** is the American conductor, record producer and film composer who, to date, has received no less than 79 Grammy Award nominations.

Jones, who worked as arranger for Frank Sinatra's 1964 *Swing* album, is also noted as producer of the late Michael Jackson albums *Thriller* and *Off the Wall*.

In the world of rock, **John Paul Jones** is the musician, songwriter and arranger who was born John Baldwin in 1946 in Sidcup, Kent.

Best known as the bassist and keyboardist for the British rock band Led Zeppelin, he now pursues a successful solo career as a musician and producer.

Born in Manchester in 1945, **Davy Jones** was the singer, songwriter and actor who is best known as having been the lead vocalist from 1965 to 1971 of the pop group The Monkees, enjoying hits that include *Daydream Believer* and *Last Train to Clarksville*.

He died in 2012, while in a different musical genre **Aled Jones** is the Welsh classical singer who was born in 1970 in Bangor.

Only fifteen years old when he recorded the best-selling *Walking in the Air*, the theme from the animated film *The Snowman*, he is also noted as the presenter of BBC TV's *Songs of Praise*.

Best known for her recording in 1964 of *Tainted Love*, a major hit in later decades for British band Soft Cell, **Gloria Jones** is the American singer and songwriter who was born in 1945 in Cincinnati.

She had been romantically involved with the British pop star Marc Bolan when, in September of 1977, the car she was driving was involved in a road accident that claimed Bolan's life.

Honoured by America's National Endowment for Arts in 1989 with its Jazz Masters Award, **Hank Jones** is the veteran jazz pianist and composer who was born in 1918 in Vicksburg, Mississippi, and who has played with such jazz greats as Ella Fitzgerald, Charlie Parker and Nancy Wilson.

Back to rock music, Kenney Jones, born in

London in 1948, is the drummer who, after playing with the Small Faces in the 1960s, joined The Who in 1979 following the death of drummer Keith Moon.

Born in 1969 in Tredegar, Wales, **Nicholas Jones**, also known as Nicky Wire, is the bassist and lyricist with Welsh rock band Manic Street Preachers, while, also in Wales but in a different musical genre, **Paul Jones** is the leading international baritone who was born in Cardiff in 1974.

Born in 1942 in Portsmouth, **Paul Jones** is the English singer, actor and musician best known as the vocalist and harmonica player with the 1960s band Manfred Mann, while **Malcolm Jones**, born in Inverness in 1959, is a musician and songwriter with Scottish band Runrig.

Described as the greatest living country singer, **George Jones** was born in 1931 in Saratoga, Texas.

Married to country singer Tammy Wynette, his many hits include the 1959 *White Lightning* and the 1983 *I Always Get Lucky With You*.

Finally in the world of music, but by no means least, David Robert Hayward Jones was the musician, record producer, arranger and actor better known as **David Bowie**.

Born in 1947 in Brixton, London, by the time

of his death in 2016 he had sold an estimated 136 million albums worldwide, including the 1969 *Space Oddity*, *The Rise and Fall of Ziggy Stardust and the Spiders from Mars*, from 1972, and the 2003 *Suburbia*.

Ranked among the ten best-selling acts in UK pop history and ranked 39th by *Rolling Stone* magazine in 2004 in its list of the 100 greatest rock artists of all time, he modestly declined a British knighthood in 2003.

From music to film, Bowie's son, **Duncan Jones**, is the film director, producer and screenwriter born Duncan Zowie Hayward Jones in Beckenham, Kent, in 1971, who directed the acclaimed 2009 *Moon*.

Married to American actor Michael Douglas since 2000, **Catherine Zeta-Jones** is the Welsh actress who was born in Swansea in 1969.

It was following roles in a number of British and American television productions that she came to international prominence in 1996 for her role in *The Phantom*, while her portrayal of Velma Kelly in the 2002 *Chicago* earned her a number of awards that include an Academy Award for Best Supporting Actress.

Born in 1946 in San Saba, Texas, **Tommy Lee Jones** is the American actor and film director whose film roles include the 1981 *The Executioner's*

Song and the 1997 *Men in Black*, while he received an Academy Award nomination for Best Actor for the 2007 *In the Valley of Elah*, and an Academy Award for Best Supporting Actor in 1993 for the *The Fugitive*, starring alongside Harrison Ford.

On the television screen, **Ruth Jones**, born in 1967 in Bridgend, Wales is the award-winning actress, comedian, singer and writer best known as one of the co-writers and stars of the popular comedy series *Gavin and Stacey*.

Born in London in 1970, **Rupert Penry-Jones** is the English actor best known for his role in the British television spy series *Spooks*, while **Terry Jones**, born in 1942 in Colwyn Bay, is the Welsh comedian, actor, author and screenwriter best known as a member of the former *Monty Python* television and film team.

Across the Atlantic, **James Earl Jones**, born in 1931 in Arkabutla, Mississippi, is the American actor and recipient of a 2009 Screen Actors Guild Lifetime Achievement Award whose films include the 1989 *Field of Dreams*, the 1990 *The Hunt for Red October* and, from 1995, *Cry, the Beloved Country*.

Born in 1947 in Stoke-on-Trent, **Freddie Jones** is the English character actor whose many film roles include the 1970 *The Man Who Haunted Himself* and, from 2004, *Ladies in Lavender*, while **Griff Rhys Jones** is the Welsh comedian, writer and television presenter who was born in Cardiff in 1953.

Known for his 1980s' British television comedy series *Alas Smith and Jones*, along with fellow comedian Mel Smith, he is also a recipient of the 1994 Laurence Olivier Theatre Award for Best Comedy Performance, for his role in the play *Absolute Turkey*.

Behind the camera lens, **Michael Caton-Jones** is the Scottish director of films that include the 1989 *Scandal*, the 1990 *Memphis Belle* and, from 2006, *Basic Instinct 2*; born Michael Jones in Broxburn, West Lothian, in 1957, he added 'Caton' to his surname after his marriage to his first wife, Beverly Caton.

Combining film with football, **Vinnie Jones**, born in 1965 in Watford, is the former English midfielder who played for teams that include Wimbledon, Leeds and Chelsea and now pursues an equally successful career as an actor.

His best known film role is the 1998 *Lock, Stock and Two Smoking Barrels*, while others include the 2000 *Snatch* and, from 2009, *Year One*.

From film and football to the golf course, **Bobby Jones**, born in 1902 in Atlanta, Georgia, has been described as one of the greatest golfers to have ever competed at both national and international level.

By the time he decided to quit the game at the age of only 28, he had achieved the unique 'Grand Slam' of winning all four major golf tournaments – the amateur and open championships in the USA and Britain – in a single year (1930).

He was inducted into the World Golf Hall of Fame three years after his death in 1971.

In the Welsh national sport of rugby, **Adam Rhys Jones**, born in 1981 in Abercrave, is the rugby union player who made his debut for the national team in 2003, while another **Adam Jones**, born in Swansea in 1980, is the lock forward who has also played for his country.

Combining rugby and athletics, **Ken Jones**, born in 1921 in Blaenavon, Monmouthshire was the Welsh international rugby union player who, as an athlete, won a silver medal in the 4x400-metres relay at the 1948 Olympics; he died in 2006.

Also on the athletics track, **Barbara Jones**, born in 1937, is the former American athlete who won a gold medal in the 4x100-metres at the 1952 Olympics and gold for the same event at the 1960 Olympics.

Bearers of the Jones name have also excelled in the creative world of literature.

Born in 1949 in Lexington, Virginia, **Gayl Jones** is the contemporary African American writer whose novels include the 1975 *Corregidora* and whose poetry includes the 1981 *Song for Anninho*, while Dennis Feltham Jones was a noted British science fiction writer.

Born in 1917 and better known as **D.F. Jones**, his futuristic 1966 novel *Colossus* was later filmed as *Colossus: The Forbin Project*, while his last novel, *Bound in Time*, was published in 1981, the year of his death.

In the realms of fantasy novels, **Diana Jones**, born in London in 1934, is the writer whose works include the *Chrestomanci* series and the 1998 *Lord of Derkholm*.

Drawing his inspiration from harrowing personal experience as a soldier, **James Jones** was the American author best known for his novels based on the Second World War.

Born in 1921 in Robinson, Illinois, he enlisted in the U.S. Army in 1939 and witnessed the Japanese attack on Pearl Harbor two years later.

This led to his first novel, the 1951 *From Here to Eternity*, which was later filmed, as was his second novel, the 1962 *The Thin Red Line*; he died in 1977.